IMAGES
of America

KINGS PARK

AERIAL VIEW OF KINGS PARK, 1936. This photograph was taken in August 1936, when the Kings Park Fire Department was sponsoring a fireman's tournament; the fire department is shown parading down Main Street. Main Street runs left to right through the center of the photograph. The view reveals how open the land was around the town and conveys the feeling that Kings Park was a country village. The Stattel farm stretches to the right around the water tower, and farther south is the Nowick Farm. The Kings Park State Hospital farm fields extend to the left. (Kings Park Heritage Museum.)

ON THE COVER: Unidentified children are shown with Fr. Gerald Gardner in "Cottage Field" on the grounds of St. Johnland in Kings Park in the spring of 1948. The facility's "Founder's Well" is visible in the background. (Richard H. Handley Collection of Long Island Americana, Smithtown Library.)

IMAGES
of America

KINGS PARK

Bradley Harris, Joshua Ruff,
and Marianne Howard

ARCADIA
PUBLISHING

Published by Arcadia Publishing
Charleston, South Carolina

Printed in the United States of America

Library of Congress Control Number: 2017931435

For all general information, please contact Arcadia Publishing:
Telephone 843-853-2070
Fax 843-853-0044
E-mail sales@arcadiapublishing.com
For customer service and orders:
Toll-Free 1-888-313-2665

Visit us on the Internet at www.arcadiapublishing.com

CONTENTS

Acknowledgments   6

Introduction   7

1.   St. Johnland   11

2.   The Kings Park Psychiatric Center   27

3.   Early Kings Park   53

4.   Churches and Schools   85

5.   Building Modern Kings Park   101

ACKNOWLEDGMENTS

This book would not be possible without the support of the Kings Park and greater Smithtown communities, so many members of which assisted us throughout the research and compilation of this book. We would like to thank Leo Ostebo, Gail Hessel, and the Board of Directors of the Kings Park Heritage Museum; Timothy T. Eagan, superintendent of the Kings Park Central School District; and the staff of the RJO Intermediate School. Your time, resources, knowledge, and patience were invaluable to us. An additional debt of gratitude goes to Miles Borden and King Pedlar, whose depth of expertise and previously written works were extremely helpful.

Much appreciation goes to Caren Zatyk, of the Richard H. Handley Collection of Long Island Americana and the Reference Department of the Smithtown Library, for repeated access to your research files and photographs. Additionally, kudos to the staff of St. Joseph's Parish, a church now celebrating its 125th year, who provided information on their history with such ease.

Finally, thanks to Pat Biacianiello, Fred Messina, Tony Tanzi, Bill and Karen Saverese, and the Hennings family for your community-centered dedication and your assistance with this undertaking.

Unless otherwise noted, all images appear courtesy of the Smithtown Historical Society.

INTRODUCTION

Before Kings Park, this area was home to the Society of St. Johnland, a utopian Christian community founded in Smithtown in 1865 by an Episcopalian priest named William Augustus Muhlenberg. Reverend Muhlenberg, pastor of the Church of Holy Communion in Manhattan and the creator of St. Luke's in New York City, worked with the poor of Manhattan during the Civil War. He dreamt about creating a refuge for members of the Protestant working class poor. He began to talk and write about creating a Christian industrial community, a rural settlement that would be a haven for crippled and destitute children, orphaned boys and girls, and indigent old men. Dr. Muhlenberg managed to convince wealthy parishioners to contribute $14,000 for the purchase of the 400-acre Abram Smith farm located on the Sound shore in Smithtown, and so began the development of the utopian community that he called the Society of St. Johnland.

By 1870, when incorporation papers were filed, Dr. Muhlenberg's dream was well on the way to becoming a reality. Cottages had been built and tenanted by deserving families, a home for crippled and destitute children had been opened, and an inn for old men had been completed. The following year, more buildings were added to the property—a house for boys, an extension of St. John's Inn with accommodations for 10 orphaned girls, and the original farmhouse, which was renovated and enlarged to serve as living quarters for the superintendent and guests. The settlement became a thriving community.

In 1873, when the Long Island Rail Road (LIRR) extended its North Shore branch from Northport to Port Jefferson, the railroad created a station at the crossroads of North Country Road and Indian Head Road, and they named the station St. Johnland, which seemed appropriate, since the settlement contained the largest concentration of people living in the area, which was rapidly becoming a little rural village. On January 13, 1873, when the first LIRR train ran through St. Johnland station, there were only a few homes in the immediate area. Most people getting off the train were headed to St. Johnland.

The community around the railway station changed dramatically in 1885. That year, the Kings County Board of Supervisors, with the sanction of the New York State Legislature, purchased 873.8 acres of land from the Society of St. Johnland for the establishment of a Kings County Farm to provide for the care, custody, and relief of the poor and insane of Kings County. The idea of Smithtown receiving hordes of poor and "insane" patients did not sit well with the residents, and a committee was formed to look after the interest of the town, although their efforts were doomed, since the decision to allow the purchase of the farm property had already been made in Albany.

After 1885, the committee shifted its attention from seeking to stop the establishment of the Kings County Farm to making sure that the institution paid its full share of taxes. In this endeavor, they were successful. In 1888, a final determination was made by the Albany legislature that the town could assess the Kings County Farm an annual tax bill of "One Hundred and Fifty thousand dollars."

By 1892, the Kings County Farm was receiving and treating over 1,000 patients per year. The farm had several name changes and was known successively as the St. Johnland Branch Asylum, the Branch of Kings County Lunatic Asylum, and, finally, the Long Island State Hospital at Kings Park when it became a state institution on October 1, 1896.

The establishment of the Kings County Farm had a profound impact on the tiny hamlet. People moved into the community with the thought of working at the hospital or starting businesses, and stores, hotels, livery stables, restaurants, taverns, and boardinghouses opened. The transformation of St. Johnland was completed in 1891, when the name of the railroad station was changed from St. Johnland to Kings Park. The community that had once been dependent upon the institution of St. Johnland for its survival was now dependent upon the institution that became known in 1905 as the Kings Park State Hospital.

The Kings County Farm was meant to be a working farm where patients could perform farm work and derive therapeutic benefits. By 1900, the patient population of the Long Island State Hospital at Kings Park numbered 2,697. The hospital employed a professional staff of 10 physicians and 16 nurses. The federal census of 1900 revealed that 70 percent of the patients were foreign-born, with most of them coming from northern European countries. The patient population was served and cared for by 454 employees whose countries of origin were similar to those of the patients. The majority of the early employees were Irish: 224 members of the staff were born in Ireland. Sixty percent of these Irish employees were women, and for the most part, they were single and under the age of 30. The Irish men employed at the hospital also tended to be single, although they were older, with many of them in their 30s.

The presence of so many young, single, Irish men and women working and living on the grounds of the hospital would have a significant impact upon the community of Kings Park. As these young people became acquainted, fell in love, got married, and moved off the grounds of the hospital to find homes of their own in Kings Park, the community began to acquire a distinctly Irish population.

As the hospital steadily grew, adding buildings and patients, the town of Kings Park began to evolve. Kings Park's first business district, "the flats," was located along both sides of State Route 25A, from the entrance of Kings Park State Hospital to the railroad tracks that crossed Route 25A near the Kings Park Fire House. In this little enclave surrounded by state property, newcomers to the community established businesses that prospered. One of the first buildings constructed in the flats was the Boulevard Hotel, which was built by Eugene Keane. In 1905, Joseph Brady married Keane's daughter Marie and took over the operation of the hotel, renaming it Brady's Hotel. Brady's occupied the area that is currently the east end of the Kings Park Fire Department's parking lot.

Farther east, on the south side of Route 25A, Elias Patiky opened a dry goods store and rented to a barber named Manley Vita. Patiky built another home and store across the street. Other stores in the area included a feed store, a dry goods store, and a cigar and candy store. It was the center of town prior to 1917. But all of this changed after a tragic fire swept through the flats on May 15, 1917.

The fire is thought to have started in Vita's barbershop on the south side of Route 25A. It quickly spread to adjoining buildings, then jumped across the street, setting Patiky's store and home ablaze. Before long, the fire was raging out of control. The Kings Park Hook and Ladder Company responded with its only piece of equipment, a small hand pump mounted on a fire wagon. The fire proved to be too much for the primitive piece of equipment, and fire departments from neighboring Northport, East Northport, Smithtown, and Stony Brook responded to the call for help. Despite their best efforts, eight buildings were destroyed and a ninth was gutted. By the time the fire burned out, it had caused more than $100,000 in damage. Fortunately, no lives were lost, and it appears that no one was injured.

The fire had quite an impact upon Kings Park. People became aware of the need to have an improved fire department. In 1924, the Kings Park Fire District was established with a board of five fire district commissioners. The fire also led to the emergence of a new business district on

Upper Broadway (Route 25A west of Indian Head Road). This area became the new heart of the town and was soon packed with businesses catering to the needs of visitors and residents.

By 1917, Kings Park had become a village with some 300 homes, 20 businesses, two churches, a school, and a railroad station. World War I brought change to Kings Park. The proximity of the newly constructed Brindley Flying Field in Commack was followed by the imposition of prohibition within a 10-mile radius of the airfield. Illegal but hidden sales of liquor and beer in Kings Park continued through the pursuits of rum runners, bootleggers and speakeasies in the village.

When World War I began, many young men from Kings Park volunteered or were drafted. Some men, like William T. King, never saw combat and died at Camp Upton during the influenza epidemic of 1917. Others, like Donald C. Munro, died in combat on June 18, 1918, while fighting in France. Many men returned from the war with disabling wounds and troubling mental problems. In 1927, New York State, recognizing the need to do more for veterans, established the Kings Park Veterans Memorial Hospital on the grounds of the Kings Park State Hospital. This hospital was unique in that it was the only state-operated facility created specifically for the care of mentally-ill veterans. By the 1930s, the Kings Park hospitals had a combined patient population of over 11,000.

The Great Depression brought hard times to everyone, including the residents of Kings Park. But the presence of the Kings Park State Hospital helped to mitigate the worst aspects of the Depression, as many area residents found employment there. Employment opportunities were almost endless—the hospital hired physicians and nurses to work on its wards; skilled craftsmen to work in its electrical, machine, plumbing, sheet metal, radio, appliance, carpentry, locksmith, heating, air conditioning, painting, welding, and mason's shops; and a legion of laborers to work on the farm and perform the maintenance of the buildings and grounds.

When the Japanese bombed Pearl Harbor, the United States was once again involved in a world war, and the little village of Kings Park, with a population of 2,464 in 1940, felt the impact. Food, fuel, clothing, and tires were rationed. People volunteered to serve as enemy aircraft spotters in the tower erected at the Kings Park bluff. So many men were drafted that a shortage of manpower was felt at the state hospitals, which instituted a six-day workweek with longer shifts to provide coverage. Four years of combat claimed the lives of 11 men from Kings Park who made the ultimate sacrifice. The town would experience dramatic changes with the population surge that came after the war.

Today, the town of Kings Park has an estimated population of over 17,000. Drawn by its location near the Long Island Sound, its proximity to the LIRR and major traffic arteries leading into the metropolitan area, its excellent schools, and its suburban lifestyle, families have found homes in Kings Park. With residential developments now encroaching on the last open spaces in Kings Park, the community has reached a turning point, and planners are discussing the redevelopment of Kings Park and the need to revitalize the area. The results of these efforts will write the next chapter in the history of Kings Park.

One

St. Johnland

Authors Bradley Harris and King Pedlar described St. Johnland as "A Forgotten Utopia," founded as a safe haven, orphanage, and school for impoverished boys from Manhattan and Brooklyn. William Augustus Muhlenberg's purchase of 500 acres of woodland in 1866 grew into a campus built a stone's throw from the picturesque mouth of the Nissequogue River to the Long Island Sound. It included a camp, a home for girls, an infirmary, a baby shelter, and a living facility for seniors. Fond memories of past students, brothers, sisters, teachers, superintendents, nurses, and friends are exhibited—almost like a yearbook—in this chapter. Prior classmates are now lifelong friends who still organize reunions, write letters to one another, and reminisce about the place that was a bright star in their lives.

In the 1950s, the trustees of St. Johnland had to decide upon which community they would focus their resources, and the St. Johnland board voted to specialize in care for the elderly population. In 2016, St. Johnland celebrated its 150th anniversary; it is now a premier nursing home with specialties in dementia care, adult day health care, and rehabilitation services.

MOUTH OF THE NISSEQUOGUE, C. 1965. The Nissequogue River makes its way northward from the hills of the Ronkonkoma Terminal Moraine in Hauppauga to the Long Island Sound at the bluff in Kings Park, a distance of about four miles. The shallow riverbed restricted the passage of large sailing vessels and meant river traffic consisted of small sloops and schooners.

HIGH TIDE AT KINGS PARK, C. 1965. Obadiah Smith was the first Smith to build a home west of the Nissequogue River. When he visited his family on the east side, he would take a shortcut along the river at low tide. At high tide, this trip would be 10 to 12 miles on a wagon. This place is called the "going-over."

AERIAL VIEW OF KINGS PARK, C. 1965. Historians estimate that 6,000 Native Americans lived on Long Island when European settlers arrived. Those who lived along the Nissequogue River, including in the area where the river meets the Long Island Sound, were named the Nessequake. Today, these areas include Sunken Meadow State Park, the Society of St. Johnland, and the abandoned Psychiatric Center. The marshland is home to thousands of birds and animals, including fox, geese, osprey, owls, gulls, ducks, and herons.

OBADIAH SMITH HOUSE, C. 1880. This house is said to have been built by Obadiah Smith (1687–1765), the grandson of Richard Smythe, after his marriage to Susannah Stephens in 1708. Today, it stands in its original location on the north side of St. Johnland Road, facing south to take advantage of the southern light exposure. It contains a mixture of Dutch and English architecture.

INTERIOR OF THE OBADIAH SMITH HOUSE (UPSTAIRS BEDROOM), C. 1970. Interesting features of the interior of the house include a narrow and deep winding staircase in the entranceway, a bridge that runs from the second floor to the back end of the property, and formal bedrooms, including a fancy room with a starburst-patterned cupboard. Two bedrooms are located on the first floor, along with the kitchen, scullery, and east parlor.

WEST WALL, OBADIAH SMITH HOUSE. The west end wall has a massive beehive oven that is the back end of a large cooking fireplace that is three feet deep and eight feet wide. This fireplace is special because it is one of the largest hearths in a colonial home on Long Island.

ST. JOHNLAND SCENE, 1882. This is a reproduction of an Edward Lange painting of the area prior to the arrival of the Kings Park State Hospital. Predominantly a farming community organized in 1865, St. Johnland was set up on Sunken Meadow Road. Prominent buildings depicted here included the "Church of the Testament of Jesus," the "Cottages," and the "School House." Patients and employees from nearby hospitals were excellent customers for area farmers at that time.

SAMUEL SMITH HOUSE, C. 1920. Samuel Smith was a first lieutenant during the Revolutionary War. The history of the Head of the Harbor area begins with deeds left by Richard Smythe in 1677. In a deed, land was given to "Samuel and Adam Smith each of them 100 acres of land in stony brook neck."

CLAMBAKE ON THE NISSEQUOGUE, C. 1900. This photograph was taken at Handley's Dock. Richard M. Handley (second from left in the back row) and his wife, Mary (center of the second row in the striped blouse), owned most of what is now San Remo from St. Johnland Road to the river. Also identified in this image are Julia Lawrence (far right in the back row in black dress), Ada Strong (far left in the front row), Arthur Lawrence (boy holding straw hat in the front row), and Homer Reboul (far left in the back row).

PHOTOGRAPH FROM THE FAMILY CLAMBAKE, C. 1900. Many suggested possible sites for Muhlenberg's project, and at the end of 1865, the Smith Farm in Kings Park was brought to his attention. Many people contributed, and 200 additional acres were purchased. In the first annual report for St. Johnland, Muhlenberg describes the creation of the community, including possessing great advantages for everyone, covering an area of 400 acres, with the north boundary being Long Island Sound.

AREA THAT BECAME SUNKEN MEADOW KINGS PARK, 1911–1912. Created as a New York state park in 1928, this park takes its name from the low meadowland that separates Sunken Meadow Creek and its bordering salt marshes from the upland. The property was owned by the Lamb family, and was created with land leased from the Town of Smithtown. Originally containing 520 acres, it now encompasses over 1,200 acres. Through the 1950s, St. Johnland operated a summer camp at Sunken Meadow.

WILLIAM AUGUSTUS MUHLENBERG, C. 1860. Born in Philadelphia in 1796 to prominent German Lutherans, Muhlenberg was ordained as an Episcopalian priest in 1820 and received his Doctrine of Divinity. He founded St. Paul's, a private college near Flushing, Queens, an undertaking that brought him national and international accolades. He founded a hospital in Manhattan in honor of St. Luke. His work with the poor during the Civil War ultimately led him to think about creating a refuge for members of the Protestant working-class poor, and thus began the Society of St. Johnland.

MUHLENBERG TOMBSTONE, C. 1900. Muhlenberg died on April 8, 1877, at St Luke's Hospital. He is buried at the Society of St. Johnland. The inscription on the east side of the monument, which faces the grave, reads, "Here sleeps the earthly part of William Augustus Muhlenberg, Doctor in Divinity. He was born, September 16, 1796, ended his work, April 8, 1877." The west side of the monument reads, "I know whom I have believed."

THE GRAVE OF DR. MUHLENBERG.

ST. JOHNLAND NEAR CHESTNUT TREES, C. 1900. A sentence in the *First Annual Report*, published by the Society of St. Johnland in 1867, states, "The north boundary lies on the sound, a large part of it is a bold bluff, covered by a fine old grove of chestnut, oak, and cedar, affording it protection against northerly winds (with a) gentle slope, declining southward that forms the site of the village which is already begun." (King Pedlar Collection.)

HAVING A FINE TIME IN ST. JOHNLAND, KINGS PARK. Prior to World War I, St. Johnland flourished with the construction of shelters, an infirmary, the Muhlenberg Home for Aged Women, the Lawrence House (babies' shelter), Sunbeam Cottage, and a grammar school. Benefactors were solicited, including Cornelius Vanderbilt, to pay for construction and maintaining the facility. In spite of high costs, there were always more applicants than openings. In 1911, Alice Page Thomson became superintendent and arranged to bring 150 impoverished boys from Manhattan and Brooklyn to the beaches of St. Johnland. (King Pedlar Collection.)

POSTCARD DEPICTING A DEDICATION CEREMONY FOR THE ROBERT LOUIS HARRISON INFIRMARY, MAY 29, 1913. A crowd of staff, residents, and visitors gathered outside on the grounds of St. Johnland in Kings Park for the dedication ceremony of the Robert Louis Harrison Infirmary. The Robert Louis Harrison Infirmary was actively used as an infirmary until the mid-1950s; it later served as living quarters for some of the residents. The building burned down in 1960. (Richard H. Handley Collection of Long Island Americana, Smithtown Library.)

INTERIOR CHAPEL, 1941. The chapel replaced the original Church of the Testimony of Jesus after it was destroyed by fire in 1917. In 1922, the cornerstone was laid for St. John's Chapel, and by 1923, the chapel was back in service. When World War I began, St. Johnland contributed not only as its alumni entered the service but also by increasing crop production and caring for over 200 people throughout the war. (Gift of King Pedlar; Richard H. Handley Collection of Long Island Americana, Smithtown Library.)

SUNSET COTTAGE. The Sunset Cottage, built in 1904, was designed to be a home for older married couples, including staff at the Society of St. Johnland, as well as a final living quarters for those who had a partner buried on the grounds' cemetery. By 1912, $340 per year and per couple could ensure lodging for each of the 12 couples.

ROBERT LOUIS HARRISON INFIRMARY, 1913. When it opened, the infirmary had 16 beds, an operating room, and a dispensary with all of the latest equipment to care for both young and old. (Richard H. Handley Collection of Long Island Americana, Smithtown Library.)

ALICE PAGE THOMSON. Born in Singapore in 1868, Thomson became the superintendent of St. Johnland in 1911 and spent 35 years in service to the Society. Her concern for the health and well-being of children led to the construction of the Robert Louis Harrison infirmary, which opened in 1913. She also created the Women's Auxiliary for St. Johnland in 1915; for 40 years, this group of women provided philanthropic and physical support to the residents. (Richard H. Handley Collection of Long Island Americana, Smithtown Library.)

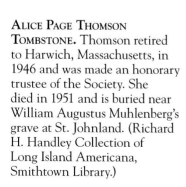

ALICE PAGE THOMSON TOMBSTONE. Thomson retired to Harwich, Massachusetts, in 1946 and was made an honorary trustee of the Society. She died in 1951 and is buried near William Augustus Muhlenberg's grave at St. Johnland. (Richard H. Handley Collection of Long Island Americana, Smithtown Library.)

SUNBEAM COTTAGE. Sunbeam Cottage, built in 1881 for the educational training of orphan girls, was paid for by Mr. and Mrs. Cornelius Vanderbilt. Following the large donation from the Vanderbilts, numerous other philanthropists donated as well, allowing the Society to continue its work for many years. The cottage had a sitting room, play room, dining room, kitchen, and dormitory space for more than 20 girls. Gloria Reynolds Foley recalls, "Every morning we would assemble there (in the playroom) for morning prayer . . . I remember, that probably, the happiest times of my childhood were spent ice skating on the pond across the road from Sunbeam House."

LAWRENCE HOUSE (THE "BABIES' SHELTER") AT THE SOCIETY OF ST. JOHNLAND, C. 1915. A babies' shelter, which provided care for children ages two through eight, was established at St. Johnland in 1892. In 1900, the Lawrence House was built to provide housing and care for these infants. This photograph shows 19 orphaned children—most of them girls—outside the house.

ENJOYING SUMMER CAMP ON ST. JOHNLAND'S PLUM ISLAND, 1935. The Society of St. Johnland had its own summer camp on an island in the Sound just north of the mouth of Sunken Meadow Creek. The older boys (ages 10–14) at St. Johnland spent the month of July on the island, staying in summer cabins, eating meals in a dining cabin, playing baseball in the morning, and swimming in the afternoon. There was always time to go clamming, crabbing, or fishing. In the early evening, a game of volleyball might be started, followed by the boys gathering around a campfire to tell scary stories and sing songs. (King Pedlar Collection.)

Boys Celebrating a Birthday at Summer Camp, St. Johnland, c. 1946. Summer camp for boys at St. Johnland was held each July until the late 1940s. This tradition was established in 1911, when superintendent Alice Page Thomson invited 150 boys to camp on the beach during the summer. Girls also took part in camp every August. One participant later remembered, "It was great fun. There were four cabins where we slept, a dining hall and a recreation cabin where Father Gardner and the camp counsellors stayed . . . the boys were split into teams for sports and jobs. We played a lot of softball and soccer and had swimming and running races." (King Pedlar Collection.)

STUART EASTMAN'S BIRTHDAY PARTY, 1948. Chisholm House was located next to Fabbri Cottage and the administration building at St. Johnland. Boys staying at the house were in grades five through eight. On February 14, 1948, Stuart Eastman (at farthest right) celebrated his 11th birthday in the dining room of Chisholm House with the other boys in the house. The cake was supplied by Eastman's mother. Housefather Arthur Winslow is the bespectacled adult in the center background. (King Pedlar Collection.)

Two

THE KINGS PARK PSYCHIATRIC CENTER

Looming over the village's horizon like moldering ruins from a lost civilization, Kings Park Psychiatric Center's remaining brick ward structures recall a time when care was provided to 10,000 patients (at the hospital's peak occupation). While the patients vastly outnumbered village residents, it was also a major engine of employment for the community, with an estimated 90 percent of townsfolk working at the 800-acre complex at its apex.

The endeavor to treat mental health patients at this location began in 1885, when the Kings County Asylum in Brooklyn chose the site—conveniently reachable by rail or boat—as the locale for a therapeutic and self-sustaining "lunatic farm." In the following decades, the Kings Park Psychiatric Center grew into a quasi-city, maintaining its own power plant, sewage treatment facility, dairy farm, and other occupational therapy operations. After years of staff and patient reductions, the hospital finally closed in 1996.

KINGS PARK STATE HOSPITAL'S POWER PLANT SMOKESTACK (ABOVE) AND THE KINGS PARK PSYCHIATRIC CAMPUS (BELOW), MAY 4, 1925. The aerial view above looks northeast towards the expanding hospital campus and the edge of the Nissequogue River. Each image illustrates the relatively fast growth of a self-sustaining operation. Since the hospital began its power plant before a public utility company even existed, by the time these photograph were taken, it featured a well-established grid for generating its own electricity. The hospital also built its own roads, sewers, steam plant, and laundry facilities.

HAND-COLORED POSTCARD, C. 1907. This hand-colored postcard depicts "a driveway" at "The Hospital, Kings Park, L.I." Mailed in 1911, it was published by Octochrome. (Richard H. Handley Collection of Long Island Americana, Smithtown Library; gift of Maggie Blanck.)

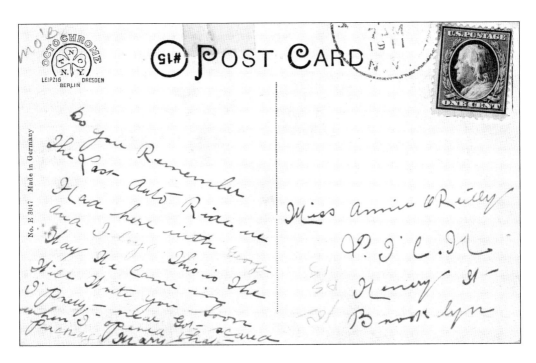

ENTRANCE ROAD TO GROUP 3 BUILDINGS, c. 1920. As this photograph indicates, the roads on the Kings Park hospital grounds were not extremely well-paved nor cared for during the early years. The Group 2 and 3 buildings were erected in 1912. They were connected by underground tunnels that allowed patients and staff to access the dining facilities.

DR. HAVILAND'S RESIDENCE, c. 1910. Housing for the hospital's staff physicians was well-appointed, as indicated by this multi-gabled house once inhabited by Dr. C. Floyd Haviland. A graduate of Syracuse University, Haviland was Kings Park's first assistant physician and served in that position for five years.

ASSISTANT SUPERINTENDENT'S HOUSE, 1911. The hospital's budget factored in interior decorating and furnishings for administrators and physicians.

DR. MACY'S RESIDENCE, C. 1908. In 1904, Dr. William Austin Macy became the hospital's superintendent, a post he held until his death in 1918. Macy oversaw the hospital's expansion and development of a strong reputation in research and treatment of mental illness. Macy also oversaw the addition of many buildings on the grounds, including 300 employee residences and clinics for the treatment of victims of typhoid and tuberculosis.

HOSPITAL GROUP 1 STRUCTURES, C. 1910. Built in the early 1900s, Group 1 structures included administrative and doctor's quarters. A series of fires destroyed many of the buildings at Group 1 in 1971.

BOULEVARD AT KINGS PARK STEWARD'S RESIDENCES, C. 1910. State law required hospital employees to live on the grounds of the Kings Park Psychiatric Center, and permission in writing was needed to travel over five miles away from the property. So the hospital built extensive housing to accommodate workers, as well as places to serve their recreational needs. Although the restrictive laws were eventually changed, housing remained available for workers who expressed an interest in living on the grounds. The steward's residence is the first building in the foreground, followed by the clubhouse, Building C (which contained male patients and the nursing school until 1919), and Building D (which contained male patients).

WARD BUILDING A, C. 1900. This was one of four structures—Ward Buildings A, B, C, and D—that were completed in 1897 and followed an identical floor plan. These patient structures offer a sharp contrast to the Kings Park Psychiatric Hospital brick towers built in the 1930s. Patients in the early ward buildings lived in single rooms in a U-shaped structure, not wide open wards with beds side by side. Administrative offices and the phone switchboard were also located in this structure. The building housed female patients until it was destroyed by fire in 1971.

FEMALE TUBERCULAR GROUP BUILDINGS, 1925. Tuberculosis is highly contagious and communicable. Mental patients who contracted it were housed in these isolated areas. Extra windows and screened doors were provided for these structures to allow for maximum ventilation and fresh air.

WARD 51, 1915. Wards were groups of rooms for mentally ill patients that included a dormitory, bedrooms, a dayroom (for recreation), a nursing station, a treatment room, and other service areas. The wards also contained bedrooms for employees. Women and men resided in different areas separated by locked doors.

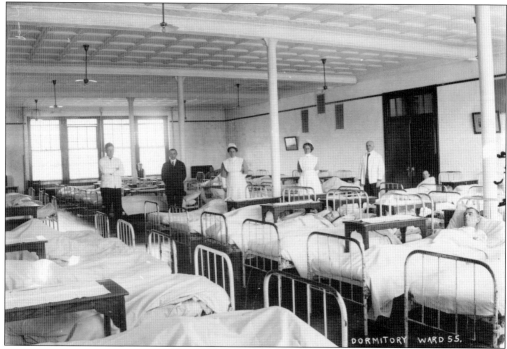

WARD 55, 1915. Beds were placed very close to one another in the wards, and a large number of infirmary patients were given around-the-clock treatment and psychiatric and nursing care.

KINGS PARK NURSING PROGRAM, CLASS OF 1917. The nursing school program at Kings Park gradually evolved. This class included six men. The woman in the center of this image (with no cap) is Ida M. Marker, who served as the principal of the School of Nursing for a long time.

NURSING CLASS, 1931. One annual report from the early years of the nursing school indicated that students learned "nursing in all its aspects," with curriculum including "anatomy, physiology, hygiene, dietetics, administration of medicines, hydrotherapy, massage, local application, surgical care of the insane, etc."

DEWING HOME FOR NURSES AND EMPLOYEES, C. 1910. The first training school for hospital employees opened in 1897. The school would eventually become the Kings Park State Hospital's School of Nursing. Enrollment grew each year. Students learned activities such as applying external medicine, hydrotherapy, preparing operating rooms, and other direct care roles.

SOLARIUM, C. 1910. A solarium located in Building Group 1 provided a beautiful and well-appointed setting for a variety of recreational activities, including dances. It was built within the curved connecting corridor between ward buildings. Windows with southern exposure provided brilliant light for the arrangement of flourishing plants.

INFORMAL PARTY GIVEN FOR WOMEN'S OCCUPATION CLASS IN SOLARIUM, 1915. This photograph shows a recreational activity at Kings Park State Hospital. In 1912, Superintendent Dr. William Austin Macy recognized the importance of recreational programs and stated in his annual report that occupying the patients' minds through diversion of activity was the only way to stimulate their minds to recovery. Initially, basketry and craft classes were introduced to patients, with other forms of amusement soon following.

WOMEN'S PHYSICAL CULTURE CLASS AT THE KINGS PARK STATE HOSPITAL, C. 1912. One of the recreational activities organized for the benefit and entertainment of patients at the Kings Park State Hospital was a physical culture class. By 1912, the hospital ran daily physical training classes for men and women where patients did calisthenics or played games. Judging from the way the women in this culture class are dressed, the calisthenics appear to be mild stretching exercises.

MEN'S PHYSICAL CULTURE CLASS, C. 1925. This men's exercise class took place inside the old assembly hall at Kings Park, which had originally been a dining hall in the women's group of early wooden structures. Plays and musicals were produced and enjoyed in this same space, but the floors were cleared for patient physical activities such as the one shown here.

CENTRAL KITCHEN FOR BUILDINGS A AND B, 1921. This enormous kitchen provided food for up to 400 patients in Ward Buildings A and B. In later years, dining services would vastly increase their capacity. In the early years, the ovens operated by burning coal. Patients were involved in food preparation and service. Note the large milk jugs in the foreground of the image; the hospital made frequent use of its onsite dairy.

LAUNDRY SERVICE, FLATWORK ROOM, C. 1915. Kings Park laundry service processed thousands of bed linens, tablecloths, and garments (both staff and patient). In earlier years, many patients were required to work here due to the intense amount of handwork —ironing, sorting, etc.—required. In the 1950s, Kings Park built a three-story laundry with chutes that could process an enormous amount of laundry in one place and required fewer laundry employees.

SEWING ROOM AT WARD 43, 1925. The hospital's self-sufficiency was famed around Long Island's North Shore. A sewing room on the premises was used for the production and repair of doctors' surgical gowns, bed linens, and patient clothing. Patients who worked in this and other rooms like it were seen as training in and gaining work skills that would aid in their recovery and occupations in the outside world.

TYPEWRITING AND STENOGRAPHY IN WARD 56, C. 1930. Occupational therapy provided possibilities for patients to achieve new skills and train for vocations that they might practice upon future release.

WOODSHOP, C. 1920. In the early 1900s, Kings Park hospital administration began embracing occupational therapy. The belief—common to both the local hospital and to other mental health administrators nationwide—was that work would provide an outlet and occupational training to assist in a patient's recovery. In 1911, 818 men and 885 women (out of 3,488 patients) were employed at Kings Park in trades ranging from masonry to basketmaking to laundry to groundskeeping.

CARPENTRY SHOP, C. 1925. Extensive carpentry and woodworking options were available for patients. Activities included furniture making (rattan and other wooden furnishings), toy and dollhouse production, and the creation of other types of wooden objects.

METAL SHOP, C. 1915. Originally Kings Park's water pumping plant, this building was later converted to the hospital's metal shop. Patients who worked here shaped and created iron products that were heated in the forge shown in the back left corner of this photograph. They made a variety of metalwork for use by both the hospital and the public at large: architectural elements, household items (like the andirons and racks shown in this photograph), and other objects.

SAWMILL, 1917. Crews at Kings Park cleared the land for cultivation, first stripping some of the wooded areas and making use of a portable sawmill that relied on donkeys to assist in the processing of the trees. Wood was used in some of the campus's structures for siding on outdoor pavilions and other temporary hospital buildings.

Cows Grazing, c. 1920. The hospital's farm area—which included a barn, silos, a milk house, and several other structures—was located along Old Dock Road. The hospital received a significant source of income from the 80 head of cattle and other livestock they kept, and the farm also benefited the patients who tended the animals.

Within the photograph:

KINGS PARK, N.Y.

SERIES OF VIEWS SHOWING CONDITION OF

"DAIRY ROAD" FROM SHERIDANS CORNER TO

ENTERANCE OF GROUP 3.   PHOTOS APR. 2. 25.

VIEW NO. 1 FROM SHERIDANS CORNER.

DAIRY ROAD FROM SHERIDAN'S CORNER, 1925. This photograph offers a side view of the fenced-in edges of the dairy farm at Kings Park, where dairymen and dairy laborers maintained a good-sized herd of milk cows.

RESERVE BATTALION CLEARING LAND, 1917. The Long Island Food Reserve Battalion was formed in early 1917 to assist the national war effort by conserving and creating food. Prominent members of the regional community were involved in the battalion, including Ralph Peters, its president, who was also president of the Long Island Rail Road. In one of its projects, the battalion cleared land for crops at the Kings Park State Hospital.

KINGS PARK HOSPITAL FOOD BATTALION CLEARS LAND, 1917. William K. Vanderbilt II of Centerport donated tractors—like the one shown here—to many large-scale land clearing operations across Long Island during World War I. The work at Kings Park was difficult, requiring the removal of a variety of woodland trees, stumps, and vegetation in order to clear the land for planting.

PICKING PEAS, 1917. Teams of patients often worked, overseen by uniformed attendants, in the fields on vegetable care and production. The pea crop alone totaled 2,834 pounds in 1914.

"A GOOD STAND OF TIMOTHY," 1918. Illustrative of the self-sufficiency of the Kings Park operation, this photograph shows a field of timothy being harvested in midsummer for use in livestock care. In addition to timothy, the Kings Park farm fields grew an astonishing variety of produce ranging from asparagus to horseradish to turnips.

SPRAYING POTATOES, 1917. Over the course of World War I, the hospital's crop production rose dramatically—from a $14,577 value in 1916 to a $40,554 value in 1918. The steward of the hospital reported that by early 1917, hospital staff had placed "all available forces at work in preparing land" for crop production.

POTATOES AND CORN, 1917. A large number of hospital patients worked for Kings Park vegetable farming operations, especially during harvest time. Even more patients worked in the fields during World War I, when food shortages prompted the federal government to ask all hospitals to clear as much farmland and grow as many crops as possible.

HARVESTING WHEAT
STATE HOSPITAL, KINGS PARK, N.Y.
JULY 26, 1917.

HARVESTING WHEAT AT THE KINGS PARK STATE HOSPITAL ON JULY 26, 1917. World War I began for the United States on April 2, 1917, with Pres. Woodrow Wilson's war message to Congress. Americans everywhere were asked to make sacrifices and contribute to the war effort by helping to bolster food reserves. Locally, the Long Island Food Reserve Battalion initiated a campaign to bring more land under cultivation. The Kings Park State Hospital put all available forces to work in clearing and preparing land for planting food crops. Lawns were plowed and planted to make room for the planting of potatoes or wheat. This photograph shows a team of three horses harvesting wheat on what may have previously been a grassy lawn. The effort paid off with an increase in the total acreage under cultivation on the hospital grounds from 141 acres in 1916 to 169 acres in 1917.

48

THE PIGGERY, C. 1917. Pigs were given leftover dining hall scraps and were fairly easy to care for. This piggery contained a sizable number of livestock: a total of 725 pigs were in the pens at Kings Park by September 1917. The pigs were raised for consumption at the hospital (a slaughterhouse and meat storage facility was also on site) and were cared for by patients.

FIRE ENGINES, C. 1925. The hospital had numerous fire vehicles and apparatuses as well as a sizable team of firemen to protect the large community and their properties. In the 1920s, the fire department grew to include a hook and ladder truck, a pumper, and a chief's car.

FIRE BURNING WARD BUILDINGS A, B, C, AND D, 1971. As patient releases increased, more buildings on the Psychiatric Hospital campus became abandoned and subject to vandalism. A series of fires in 1971 destroyed many of the 10 buildings in Group 1.

KINGS PARK PSYCHIATRIC HOSPITAL MAINTENANCE STAFF, 1958. Many changes occurred in the hospital during the 1950s and 1960s. The board closed farm operations in 1950, as they had become economically unfeasible. The hospital began to treat patients with psychotropic drugs in 1954, and while the patient population peaked at 10,000 in 1955, it began to decline soon after. Even as the patient population declined, the hospital remained a major source of employment in the area.

ALZHEIMER'S AND HEAD TRAUMA CARE UNIT, 1994. As the hospital's operations drew to a close and it released patients in a steady stream, several new, small-scale service operations began to operate on the former grounds in the 1990s, including this facility.

BUILDING 93, KINGS PARK PSYCHIATRIC CENTER HOSPITAL. Starting in 1968, thousands of patients at Kings Park and other state hospitals began to be released, a trend that continued up until the hospital's closure in 1996. In years after, this shuttered brick edifice, Building 93—now obsolete, unsafe, and a magnet for vandals—became the decaying symbol of a past age as questions persisted about its future demolition. (King Pedlar Collection.)

Three

EARLY KINGS PARK

The name "Kings Park" was first applied to a railway station on the Long Island Rail Road (LIRR) in 1891. The station was a stop on the LIRR branch line running from Northport to Port Jefferson. That branch line opened in 1873, and the railroad initially chose the name "St. Johnland" for the station that is today Kings Park because there was nothing in the area that the railroad passed through except several large farms. The closest thing to a village was the little settlement of the Society of St. Johnland, which was located some four miles away from the station.

The area around the train station was very slow to develop, and 15 years passed before a significant number of homes were built near the station. In 1885, Kings County purchased 873.8 acres of land from the Society of St. Johnland for the establishment of a working farm that Kings County could use for the care, custody, and relief of the poor and mentally ill. Kings County moved quickly to establish the farm; by 1892, the county had constructed four large buildings and 30 cottages to receive and treat more than 1,000 patients per year.

This activity on farmland northeast of the LIRR station led to the construction of businesses and residences. A hotel, a general store, a livery stable, a funeral parlor, a dry goods store, a cigar store, and a candy store opened in a newly created business district along Route 25A in the area known as the "flats." By 1917, Kings Park had evolved into a village of 300 homes, some 20 businesses, two churches, a school, a railroad station, and its own hook and ladder company.

What began as St. Johnland had morphed into Kings Park, a vibrant little village that was sustained by the presence of the Long Island State Hospital. Its future was filled with promise.

COMMUTERS WAITING TO BOARD THE TRAIN, C. 1891. From Kings Park Station, it was a 43.88-mile trip to Long Island City. These men waiting for the train to Long Island City are outfitted in bowler hats, vests, and ties and appear to be foremen or supervisors on their way to work in the city. (King Pedlar Collection.)

A Steam Locomotive Arrives at the St. Johnland Railroad Station in 1891. The station was built in 1872 and opened in January of 1873, when service on the branch line began. The Long Island Rail Road (LIRR) named it St. Johnland so that people would know where to get off the train if they wished to visit the Society of St. Johnland. In 1872, there were only a couple of farms in the surrounding area, and the railroad station was quite isolated. However, it was not long before a small community began to form around the railroad station and along North Country Road. In 1885, when Kings County purchased land from the Society of St. Johnland and created the Kings County Farm and Asylum northeast of the railroad station, more people moved into the area as the Kings County institution grew. In 1891, the LIRR renamed the railroad station Kings Park.

THE BROOKLYN HOTEL, BUILT IN 1892 BY GEORGE CUSICK. Cusick was a New York City fireman who moved to Kings Park in 1881. He initially built a hotel on the southwest corner of Pulaski Road and Route 25A, but that building was destroyed by fire. He then built a hotel near the railroad station, naming it the Brooklyn Hotel after the old Brooklyn Hotel in New York City. The hotel flourished, and its tavern and restaurant did well until the 1920s, when Prohibition hurt the business and the Cusisks sold the hotel. The old hotel still looks remarkably like it did when it was first built, except the open porches have all been enclosed to create interior space for the Long River Chinese Restaurant. (Kings Park Heritage Museum.)

THE L.W. LAWRENCE HOUSE. This house was located on Landing Road in Kings Park around 1920. (Richard H. Handley Collection of Long Island Americana, Smithtown Library.)

"SUMMER BUILDING." Part of the L.W. Lawrence Estate, the "Summer Building" was located on Landing Road in Kings Park around 1920. (Gift of T. Dempsey; Richard H. Handley Collection of Long Island Americana, Smithtown Library.)

THE SAN REMO SECTION OF KINGS PARK, C. 1920. The area shown here is near Violet Road looking toward the Nissequogue River. (Gift of T. Dempsey; Richard H. Handley Collection of Long Island Americana, Smithtown Library.)

PHOTOGRAPH OF THE NISSEQUOGUE RIVER, C. 1920. This vantage point looks east from Walnut Road and Riviera Drive in the San Remo section of Kings Park. (Gift of T. Dempsey; Richard H. Handley Collection of Long Island Americana, Smithtown Library.)

WEST DRIVE AND MEADOW ROAD, C. 1910. This photograph features two well-known thoroughfares in Kings Park. (Gift of T. Dempsey; Richard H. Handley Collection of Long Island Americana, Smithtown Library.)

KINGS PARK ROAD, 1909. This road was named for the town of Kings Park. (Richard H. Handley Collection of Long Island Americana, Smithtown Library.)

LOOKING NORTH UP INDIAN HEAD ROAD TOWARD THE BROOKLYN HOTEL. This photograph must have been taken in the late 1930s or early 1940s. Although sidewalks had been installed, Indian Head Road was still a dirt road, and the Kings Park firehouse had yet to be expanded. (Kings Park Heritage Museum.)

LOWER BROADWAY, 1905, VIEW TO THE WEST FROM ELIAS PATIKY'S STORE. Farther to the west, beyond Patiky's dry goods store, is the building that housed John Cusick's Undertaker's Shop. Brady's Hotel is on the south side of the street. (Kings Park Heritage Museum.)

LOWER BROADWAY LOOKING EAST PAST BRADY'S HOTEL ON THE RIGHT. Eugene Keane built his hotel in 1885, when he first settled in Kings Park and opened a saloon and hotel on the south side of Route 25A. In 1905, Joseph Brady married Keane's daughter Marie and took over the operation of the saloon and hotel, renaming it Brady's Hotel. The building in the foreground at left is Mike Patiky's Auto Accessory store, with gasoline pumps standing in front. Beyond Mike Patiky's store is John J. Cusick's Undertaker's Shop. (Kings Park Heritage Museum.)

Brady's Hotel, c. 1912. This photograph shows the hotel that replaced the original Brady's Hotel, which had burned down. Joseph Brady rebuilt the hotel with a wraparound porch. He later sold this hotel to an Irishman named Cassidy, then opened another hotel—which he named the Soundview Hotel—at the bluffs. Brady later bought back the hotel from the Cassidy family and, for a while, had two hotels. (King Pedlar Collection.)

The Cusick Livery Stable. The stable was built in 1898, when George Cusick's fourth son, John J. Cusick, began a livery business in the flats. John was just 19 years old when he opened the first livery stable in the area. He began with one horse and built up the business, eventually owning 35 horses and two specially-built horse-drawn stages capable of seating 60 passengers. John's livery stable prospered, since he provided transportation for visitors to the Kings Park State Hospital and St. Johnland. (Kings Park Heritage Museum.)

JOHN CUSICK WITH HIS CHEVROLET IN FRONT OF THE CUSICK FUNERAL HOME ON LOWER BROADWAY. Just as John started the livery business, he also started the Cusick family's funeral business. In 1907, John attended an undertaker's school and graduated with a license. He then opened a new business as "John J. Cusick, Undertaker and Embalmer," and rapidly cornered the market for funerals. John was Episcopalian and took care of Protestant funerals, while the Claytons took care of Catholics. Cusick was a short, stocky Irishman with a friendly manner, and he was liked and respected by the people of Kings Park. He always said that you "had to be tough to survive in an Irish town." (Kings Park Heritage Museum.)

LOWER BROADWAY LOOKING EAST FROM THE KINGS PARK STATE HOSPITAL ENTRANCE, 1910. The buildings shown here on the south side of Broadway were lost in the 1917 fire. Only Brady's Hotel survived, and the front porch of the hotel is visibly jutting out beyond the storefronts. On the north side of the street, only the Cusick Funeral Home and the Cusick Livery Stable remained standing after the fire.

KINGS PARK BUSINESS SECTION DESTROYED BY FIRE, MAY 15, 1917. The community's first fire truck was a primitive fire wagon operated by manpower and pulled to a fire by whatever means were at hand. It was not properly equipped to handle a major fire, and the flats, the business section

pictured here, was destroyed in the fire. Eight stores were destroyed, and a ninth was gutted. A number of families were left homeless. By the time the fire burned itself out, it had done over $100,000 in damage. Fortunately, no lives were lost, and no one was injured.

DOWLING HOMESTEAD IN SAN REMO. In 1892, Patrick Dowling came to Kings Park, where he found work as a blacksmith at the Kings Park State Hospital. It was there that he met Nora Shannahan, who was working as a nurse's aide. They were married in 1895 and built this home in San Remo that overlooked the Nissequogue River. The Dowlings raised their three children—Cornelius, Thomas, and Nora—here. In 1920, after waiting forever for electric service to be extended along St. Johnland Road, the Dowlings moved into the village of Kings Park.

CARLSON HOMESTEAD. The Carlson family built this home on the south side of Main Street around 1907. The Carlson family owned concrete and construction firms that helped build the RJO School, many of the buildings on the grounds of the Kings Park State Hospital, and Sunken Meadow State Park. The Carlsons also invented and manufactured the round concrete cesspool ring with beveled slots that is still widely used today. The Carlson Homestead was one of the larger and more elegant homes in Kings Park. The house was restored in 2003. (David Flynn.)

CARLSON LUMBER YARD. The area occupied by the concrete cesspool rings became the LIRR parking lot for the Kings Park Railroad Station. The Carlson House is visible just beyond the rings. The house with triangular peaks faces Broadway. (King Pedlar Collection.)

SEN. GEORGE THOMPSON, 1864–1940. George L. Thompson was born in Smithtown on November 22, 1864. He grew up in a house on Indian Head Road near the St. Johnland railroad station. The Thompson family owned and operated a general store that stood next door, and George eventually inherited the business and ran it for 38 years. He is primarily remembered for his years of public service as a legislator for the State of New York. He was first elected in 1909 as a member of the State Assembly from Suffolk County, and he served until 1912. In 1914, he was elected to the state senate from the First Senatorial District, and he was reelected and continuously served as a state senator until his death in 1941. (Miles Borden.)

SEN. GEORGE THOMPSON HOUSE. This house, built in 1872 shortly after the railroad station was constructed, was located on the east side of Indian Head Road, south of the railroad tracks. State senator George L. Thompson lived here until 1904, when he moved into a new house on Old Dock Road near the Methodist church. Around the time Indian Head Road was widened in 1960, a two-story brick extension was added to the front of the house. (David Flynn.)

GUS KOHR'S NORTH SHORE HOTEL. Augustus "Gus" Kohr was a German immigrant who came to America in 1885. He became a naturalized citizen in 1890 and soon after found his way to Kings Park, where he purchased the home of J.W. Blydenberg. The house stood on a hill overlooking the Sunken Meadow and was located on Sunken Meadow Road just east of where the parkway overpass now stands. In 1911, Kohr created a hotel by doubling the size of the house, adding a two-and-a-half-story wing with wraparound porches.

THE FANCY "NEW YORK CITY" BAR. Gus Kohr constructed this bar in 1911 for his North Shore Hotel. With 21 rooms, the hotel received guests who came to Kings Park to visit patients at the Kings Park State Hospital or to enjoy the recreational opportunities the area offered, including hiking, fishing, boating, sailing, swimming, and hunting. After a day of outdoor fun, guests were ready for a cocktail at the bar.

SNAPPER FISHING OUTSIDE THE SUNKEN MEADOW, 1900. Located near the mouth of Sunken Meadow Creek, this was a favorite spot for fishermen; here, the freshwater from the creek mixed with the saltwater from the Sound, and fish teemed in the water.

CASTING OFF IN KINGS PARK, C. 1900. Tyler's Dock, located at the end of Kohr Road, was a favorite spot for fishermen, since it provided access to Sunken Meadow Creek and some great fishing holes near the mouth of the Nissequogue River. Tourists visiting Kings Park and staying at the North Shore Hotel enjoyed the fishing in the area.

KINGS PARK BASEBALL TEAM TAKING ON THE PHILADELPHIA GIANTS, 1913. Sometimes, the hospital squad would take on professional baseball teams such as the Philadelphia Giants. Games were played on Saturday afternoons at the hospital's baseball park as hundreds of patients watched. (King Pedlar Collection.)

KINGS PARK BASEBALL TEAM, 1916. The Kings Park baseball team was sponsored by the Kings Park State Hospital and recruited local players for the team. The Kings Park squad played other amateur clubs from the area, including Willy Collier's baseball team of actors from St. James, a team from Central Islip State Hospital, and teams from the New York City Police and Fire Departments. Pictured here are members of the 1916 Kings Park State Hospital team.

STEPS LEADING FROM THE SOUNDVIEW HOTEL TO THE BEACH ALONG THE NISSEQUOGUE RIVER. These steps made access to the beach easy, but the beach on the river was not a place to go swimming. The current was too strong, and the sewers from the hospital emptied into the canal just to the south of this beach. Guests who used the stairs wanted to go across to the town's Short Beach on the other side of the river. On Short Beach, people could change into their bathing suits in the bathhouse, swim in the Sound, or jump off the dock in the river. As a boy just before World War I, Bob Brady would row hotel guests across the river in one of the rowboats that his family kept on the riverside beach. So many people did this on a Sunday that Bob, who made 5¢ per trip, remembered days that he made over 100 trips in his rowboat, earning over $10 for his effort.

THE SOUNDVIEW HOTEL, C. 1920. The Soundview Hotel stood on the bluff overlooking the mouth of the Nissequogue River, Short Beach, and the Sound. It was located to the south of the Old Dock Restaurant on the ridge of land beyond the private bungalows and cottages in the area today. The hotel was built at the turn of the 20th century to provide lodging for people who came to see patients in the hospital. When the Brady family acquired the hotel prior to World War I, many of the guests were hospital attendants who wished to get away from it all and found the charge of $1 a night within their meager means. Lunches were usually sandwiches, while dinners were more involved, and people ordered from a limited menu. This building was razed in the 1920s.

SAN REMO, 1925. An unidentified Italian American family is shown enjoying the riverside area community five short years after it was purchased by Generoso Pope, the owner of *Il Progresso*, an Italian American newspaper. Italian American residents of Brooklyn frequently used the area as a summertime recreational community for the next 30 years.

THE CLARK HOUSE, C. 1930. This house was located at Rosewood Road and Violet Road in the San Remo section of Kings Park. (Gift of T. Dempsey; Richard H. Handley Collection of Long Island Americana, Smithtown Library.)

KINGS PARK NATIONAL BANK ON THE NORTHWEST CORNER OF ROUTE 25A AND CHURCH STREET. This photograph captures opening day of the bank in 1924. A group of musicians is seated by the bank's entrance to welcome new customers. It is also apparent that the building was still being finished, as painters are shown working on the last office on the north end of the building.

LOOKING EAST ALONG UPPER BROADWAY, C. 1924. Just seven years after the fire in the "flats" destroyed Kings Park's fledgling business district on Lower Broadway, a new business district developed along Upper Broadway. By 1924, so many new businesses had filled in the open lots on the north and south sides of the street that the area appears congested. At the west end of the main street, where Indian Head Road crossed Broadway, a traffic light was installed to coordinate the flow of traffic through the busy intersection. Just beyond the traffic light, the new firehouse of the Kings Park Fire Department is standing vigil over the new business district.

ROULSTON'S. This was Kings Park's first chain store. In 1917, the building was owned by Elias Patiky; it was later managed by Jerry Reddy Sr. Here, Kings Park residents bought groceries on credit. Nobody had much money in those days, and cash was hard to come by between paydays, so the store accepted credit; local residents paid their bills twice per month.

JUDGE JOHN J. KELLY IN HIS LAW OFFICE ON MAIN STREET, KINGS PARK, 1934. Kelly was one of the first residents of Kings Park to purchase a home on Church Street just south of the Catholic church. Sometime around 1890, he constructed the building on Main Street to house offices for his insurance and real estate business. Judge Kelly was a respected member of the community and was elected over and over again as justice of the peace on the Republican ticket. Judge Kelly held court in his office. He rented out the second floor, which contained cold water flats. Tenants of these flats had to buy coal and wood to use in the stove provided in the rented room. There was no piped-in water, which meant that tenants had to use privies located behind the building.

KINGS PARK FIRE TRUCK, 1926. This American LaFrance pumper was the first "factory bought" fire truck acquired by the Kings Park Fire District. The truck was built in Elmira, New York, and its pumping capacity was 400 gallons per minute. It is powered by a four-cyclinder Buda engine and can move on the highway at speeds of 30–35 miles per hour. The truck has been out of service since 1962. But "the 26," as it is affectionately known, is still housed in the Kings Park firehouse and is used in parades and proudly displayed at antique fire truck musters.

THE KINGS PARK FIRE DEPARTMENT'S 1926 AMERICAN LAFRANCE. The LaFrance is shown here getting gas at Terrill's Texaco Service station at the east end of town; this site is now home to the Valero gas station on the corner of Park Avenue and Main Street. (Kings Park Heritage Museum.)

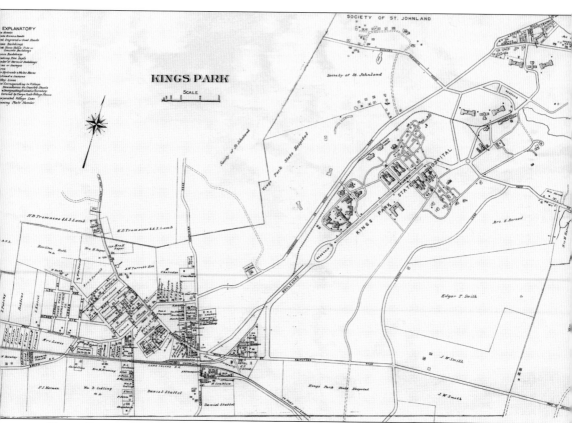

KINGS PARK MAP, 1917. This map shows the concentration of dwellings around the railroad station and the continuing development of the Kings Park State Hospital grounds. (Kings Park Heritage Museum.)

SNOWSTORM OF 1934. The blizzard of February 1934 disrupted life throughout the town. The storm dumped several feet of snow throughout the town, and highways were absolutely clogged with drifted snow. The highway department did not have any equipment that could handle the deep drifts. All they had was a wooden V-shaped plow that was pulled behind an old Adams 77 grader. It took weeks to clear the major highways, and many side streets were never plowed. Some were cleared by crews with shovels.

THREE YOUNG FELLAS. Bob Walsh (left), Harry McKee (center), and Bob Denker (enjoying an ice cream cone) are pictured on Kings Park's main street in 1938. They are on the south side of Broadway, standing in front of the building that once housed Young Brothers Appliances. (King Pedlar Collection.)

THE PARK DINER, 1946. Owned by the McWilliams family, the Park Diner was located on the southeast corner of Main Street and Renwick Avenue, across from today's Astoria Bank. Now gone, the diner was once the place to go in Kings Park for "home cooking." (King Pedlar Collection.)

YOUNG WOMEN FROM KINGS PARK. These young ladies are sitting on pilings of the "old dock" at the end of Old Dock Road. One might wonder how these young women were able to climb up on the pilings. (King Pedlar Collection.)

THE SHORELINE AT KINGS PARK BLUFF. This vantage point looks west toward the mouth of Sunken Meadow Creek and St. Johnland's Plum Island. The Society of St. Johnland had its own summer camp on Plum Island, located just north of the mouth of Sunken Meadow Creek. (King Pedlar Collection.)

THE RAIS FAMILY AT SUNKEN MEADOW STATE PARK, 1931. Sunken Meadow State Park had not been open long before the Rais family decided to visit its boardwalk and beaches.

RAIS FAMILY MEMBER IN TANK TOP, 1931. One interesting thing about this photograph is the tank top that the Rais family member is wearing. Men and boys had to wear shirts with their swimsuits, since it was against the law to bare their nipples in public.

THE VAUSE HOUSE BEING BARGED TO THE END OF OLD DOCK ROAD, 1928. This house was originally located near Tyler's Dock and was moved after the state purchased Plum Island from St. Johnland and converted the area into Sunken Meadow State Park. The Vause house was loaded onto a barge and floated to the end of Old Dock Road, where it was placed on a foundation just south of the Old Dock Inn and still stands today. (King Pedlar Collection.)

KINGS PARK POST OFFICE, C. 1940. The old post office is pictured here when it stood on the southeast corner of Meadow and Indian Head Roads. This site is now occupied by the Kings Park Florist and Anderson's Deli. The Conklin House is visible in the background. Clayton's Funeral Parlor is currently located on this corner. (King Pedlar Collection.)

Four

CHURCHES AND SCHOOLS

The churches and schools of Kings Park reflect the growth of societal demands in the town. Tidal waves of immigrants, the surge in population, and changing needs of the community combined to influence the way the populace assembled, worshipped and studied.

Among the buildings of Kings Park, churches and schools represent the philanthropic nature and closeness of its people—a strong appreciation felt throughout the hamlet that can still be perceived today.

Once having to bus their children to neighboring schools, Kings Park residents soon experienced an increase in diversity, and gradually this was no longer necessary. Even as it existed in its own enclave from the nearing towns, Roman Catholic, Protestant, Methodist, and Jewish places of worship expanded, as did private schools for these populations.

Old school buildings in Kings Park have been repurposed to not only educate students but also to house the Kings Park Heritage Museum and a rehabilitation center for seniors in the clergy. The churches and schools of Kings Park are constantly morphing and changing with its population and diversity.

METHODIST CHURCH, C. 1905. In the early 19th century, local Methodists organized church services that took place in private homes. Almost 90 years later, in 1892, the Platt family built this church, constructed in the memory of their son Lucien, who died at age 22. This small building was moved down the hill to the corner of Old Dock Road and Main Street from its original location just west of what is now Sunken Meadow State Park. In 1958, the original building was replaced.

EPISCOPAL CHURCH, ST. JOHNLAND. One of the first buildings erected at St. Johnland, the Church of the Testimony of Jesus, was built in 1869. Adam Norrie, a close friend of Dr. William Muhlenberg, funded this project. Until it was destroyed by a fire in 1916, this chapel was a focal point of life at St. Johnland.

Present-Day Chapel at St. John's Episcopal. Today, St. Johnland is a nonprofit, nonsectarian facility offering residents skilled nursing care in rehabilitation, Alzheimer's and dementia care, head injury rehabilitation, and home health and subacute care. The chapel remains a pivotal place of religious observance for St. Johnland residents and visitors.

THE HOWARD ORPHANAGE. Indian Park Farm was run by the Jewish Agricultural and Industrial Aid Society in 1910, when plans were being organized to sell the 500-acre parcel to the Howard Orphanage for $80,000. Shortly thereafter, 300 black orphans were moved to their new home in Kings Park. The orphanage made appeals to the local community not only for money but also donations of horses and equipment. The coal shortage during World War I proved to be too harsh for the children. After the orphanage closed, the property was given back to the Jewish Agricultural and Industrial Aid Society, which leased it to the Russian Commissioner of Agriculture.

ORIGINAL PATIKY STREET SYNAGOGUE. The first generation of the Jewish population in Kings Park was fairly Orthodox. A mikvah (ritual bath) was built in the basement of the synagogue, and it is believed to be the first one of its kind built on Long Island. The synagogue was also built with a balcony for women, which was mandatory until Leona Kleet, an active member of the congregation, decided to sit next to her husband. Sabbath services were held sporadically until the late 1930s, as most members of the synagogue were shopkeepers in Kings Park and felt they needed to keep their shops open to support their families.

KINGS PARK JEWISH CENTER. One of the earliest synagogues on Long Island, the Kings Park Jewish Center, involves the Elias and Jennie Patiky family, who moved to Dix Hills from New York City to farm in 1898. Their extended families followed shortly thereafter, and Elias's parents' house became the Jewish gathering place for families across Long Island. In 1904, the Jewish Agricultural and Industrial Aid Society bought land in Kings Park for use as a training farm for Jews. The Kings Park Jewish Brotherhood was formed with the family and the Society's forming foundation. In 1911, the Hebrew Ladies Auxiliary was formed with the Patiky family at the helm. The current synagogue, shown here, was dedicated in 1967 after the original one burned to the ground in 1964.

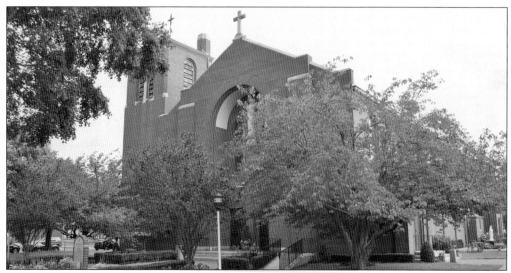

CHURCH OF ST. JOSEPH. St. Joseph's Parish, which sits at Church Street and Old Dock Road, celebrated its 125th jubilee in 2015. Charter members of St. Joseph's parish came from Ireland during the 1830s. At first, the Society of St. Johnland hosted Sunday Mass in a sun parlor of a building for its increasing numbers of Irish Catholic staff, but it soon became apparent that a Roman Catholic church needed to be formed. Kings Park established its church in 1891, and the current church was petitioned in 1953 and dedicated in 1958 by Rev. Robert J. Charpentier, Rev. Robert T. Mulligan, and Rev. James J. Hannon. Its bell tower was 56 feet tall, and its main crucifix was 10.5 feet tall.

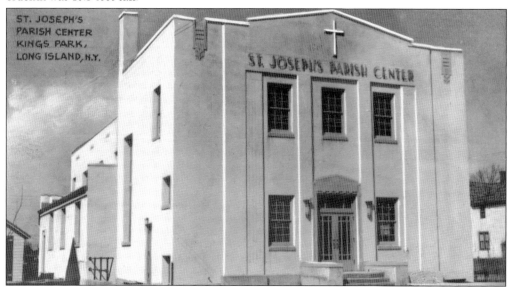

ST. JOSEPH'S PARISH CENTER. Renovated in 1951, the Parish Center provides an area outside of the church and school to meet the increasing needs of parishioners. The Parish Center housed dances, fashion shows, the confraternity recreation program for boys, the ladies auxiliary, the Blessed Virgin Sociality, the Rosary Society and the Holy Name Society. Today's ministries include the Knights of Columbus, the Catholic Daughters of America, St. Vincent de Paul Society, as well as youth ministries. St. Joseph's partnered with the Ancient Order of Hibernians in creating an outdoor shrine and plaza in honor of Our Lady of Knock, Queen of Ireland.

St. Joseph's Rectory. The first resident pastor assigned to the parish of St. Joseph's was Fr. Thomas McCaffrey in 1892. At that time, the first rectory was constructed on the same site as this present-day one. In the meantime, the rectory was a small frame house originally rented and then purchased by Father McCaffrey for $3,000. The current rectory was built between 1919 and 1920 by Rev. John I.J. Smith. St. Joseph's most recent pastor is Fr. Sean Gann, appointed in 2008; his family are also Irish immigrants who began work at Kings Park State Hospital, and he is the 16th pastor of the parish.

St. Joseph's School, 1932. This private Roman Catholic School began with an influx of Irish immigrants to the area with the development of the Society of St. Johnland. Enrollment followed the trends of other local private schools, In the early 1990s, the school expanded its facilities and programs to meet the needs of the students. In 1971, the school closed due to the increased cost of lay teachers and declining enrollment. The school building currently houses the St. Joseph's Heritage Room. (King Pedlar Collection.)

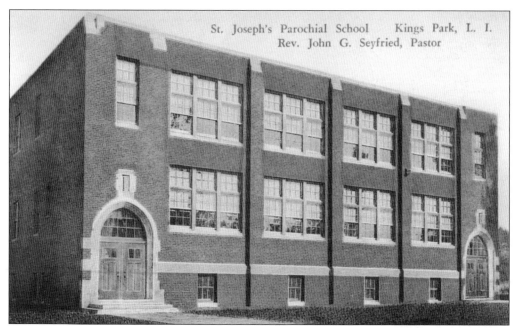

St. Joseph's Parochial School. Parishioners of St. Joseph's parish have always shown a strong commitment to Catholic education and were heartbroken when the school closed its doors in 1971. Catholic schools throughout the diocese were later reorganized in 1992, and St. Joseph's parish became one of four sponsoring schools for Holy Family Regional School in nearby Commack.

Catholic Church Interior. In 1958, a new Roman Catholic church replaced the older one in Kings Park. It is located on corner of Old Dock Road and Church Street.

KINGS PARK GRAMMAR SCHOOL, C. 1910. In 1907, a new school was constructed on Old Dock Road. After graduation, eighth-grade students would either attend Northport or Smithton High School. By 1928, the total enrollment in Kings Park Schools was 250, with a teaching staff of 8. Kings Park High School opened in 1929.

KINGS PARK SCHOOL ROOM, 1905. In 1844, a small group of residents met in the home of Gilbert S. Bryan for the purpose of organizing a school district. They elected three school trustees and approved construction of a one-room schoolhouse on Cordwood Road (now Old Dock Road). A graded elementary school opened in 1899. The Kings Park School room of Mr. Apleby is pictured here in 1905. (Kings Park Heritage Museum.)

KINGS PARK ATHLETIC ASSOCIATION, 1928–1929. Clubs, intramural sports, drama and other extracurricular activities were expanded in 1929 with the centralization of the high school; additions included a quarter-mile track, athletic fields, and a modern auditorium. (King Pedlar Collection.)

KINGS PARK HIGH SCHOOL, 1930. The first area high school opened in 1929, with grades kindergarten through 12 located in this building. There was no bus transportation at that time. In 1939, a new wing was added to the school. (King Pedlar Collection.)

KINGS PARK BOYS VARSITY BASKETBALL, 1932–1933 (ABOVE), AND KINGS PARK GIRLS VARSITY BASKETBALL, 1931–1932 (BELOW). Throughout the 1930s, there were numerous expansions in the educational offerings in the district. The community youth were offered basketball programs and leagues, and adults were offered educational classes. Expanding music and reading programs soon followed. (King Pedlar Collection.)

KINGS PARK HIGH SCHOOL GRADUATING CLASS, 1934. The school district continued to grow through the 1970s to include almost 7,000 students. (King Pedlar Collection.)

KINGSMEN MARCHING BAND, C. 1968. This photograph shows the Kings Park High School Kingsmen marching in a Memorial Day parade through the main boulevard of the Kings Park Psychiatric Hospital. The band is still appropriately named the Kingsmen. (King Pedlar Collection.)

RJO Intermediate School. Named after Ralph J. Osgood, principal of the Kings Park School in 1926, RJO is the intermediary school in Kings Park. Under Osgood's direction, the school district added gym and home economics classes during the growth of the school district. In 1928, the Kings Park Central School District was established with a total enrollment of almost 250 students and eight teachers employed. During the 1970s and 1980s, there were several calls to close this school when enrollment declined, but at that time it housed the district offices, so it remained open.

VIEWS OF ST. JOSEPH'S CHURCH AND RECTORY.

PHOTOS BY P.HILDENBRAND.

ST. JOSEPH'S ROMAN CATHOLIC CHURCH AND RECTORY, C. 1920. Built in 1898 and formally dedicated by Bishop McDonnell in 1899, the Church of Saint Joseph became the church for Catholics living in Kings Park and for many of the residents and staff members of the Kings Park State Hospital. The church took one year to build and cost $17,000. The wooden building measured 40 by 80 feet and had a seating capacity of 300. This church on Church Street served the community of Kings Park from 1899 until 1958, when it was torn down and the current St. Joseph's Parish church was erected on the same property.

Five

BUILDING MODERN
KINGS PARK

In the 1950s and 1960s, Kings Park faced stampeding homebuyers as the area's forests and waterways became the stage for the construction of brand new residential developments. A series of loose-knit neighborhoods arose within 10 square miles of the Kings Park Central School District, which saw its student population explode by nearly 400 percent between 1957 and 1965. The community's growth was also measured by a rising tax base and increasing numbers of Long Island Rail Road commuters.

"Kings Park, hilly, wooded, and well off the main route of progress . . . found itself caught in the powerful eddies of the eastward wave" of suburbia, observed the *New York Herald Tribune* in the mid-1960s. More recently, in the aftermath of the closing of the Kings Park State Hospital, Kings Parkians have embraced an ambitious downtown revitalization plan that promises to provide new affordable housing and to polish and upgrade the village's pedestrian-friendly feel.

TRAIN STATION, DECEMBER 1952. During its postwar suburban growth period, Kings Park saw the number of Long Island Rail Road (LIRR) daily commuters (with restricted monthly tickets) expand to 300 by 1965 as the population of year-round residents increased. Several years prior to when this photograph was taken, the LIRR had one of an increasing number of accidents near Kings Park on February 16, 1947, when 16 passengers were injured when the train hit an open switch and jumped the tracks. Such incidents led to increased oversight and the eventual formation of the Metropolitan Transportation Authority (MTA). (King Pedlar Collection.)

Park Auto Repair Shop on the Corner of Dawson and Main Streets. This garage was opened in 1946 and run by Pat Nasso. Following World War II, there was great demand for mechanics who could repair used cars, and Nasso filled that void. This site was later home to an Esso gas station with an attached repair shop. (King Pedlar Collection.)

Phil Baker Dances at a Kings Park Fire Department Party, c. 1955. Baker, a World War II veteran and local firefighter, enjoyed cutting a rug at an evening KPFD dinner party. With the growth of the population in the postwar years, fire district services expanded. In 1957, the department formed an Ambulance Squad. (King Pedlar Collection.)

YOUNG MEN FROM ST. JOHNLAND REUNITING IN 1963. The three men pictured here—Augie deEcheandia (left), Ralph deEcheandia (center), and Ken Jones—all attended St. Johnland Camp in their youth. They are standing next to Ralph's 1952 classic MG car in front of The Roundtable (now Shanahan's) Bar on Old Dock Road, across the street from the old Kings Park Psychiatric Center's power station. (King Pedlar Collection.)

SAN REMO ELEMENTARY SCHOOL CLASSROOM, 1965. In the 1960s, Long Island saw a drastic increase in population, growing to contain more than 1.6 million people by 1970. The suburbs had pushed well into Suffolk County, with most small homes being built on quarter-acre lots. (Kings Park Heritage Museum.)

KINGS PARK INDIAN HEAD ROAD LOOKING SOUTH, 1960. The village continued to be a residential development magnet in the early 1960s, with an average rate of 400 new homes being erected in the village each year. Most of the construction happened to the north and east of the site shown in this photograph. (King Pedlar Collection.)

AERIAL VIEW OF KINGS PARK TAKEN BY SMITHTOWN PLANNING BOARD, MAY 1966. This aerial view of Kings Park reveals the extensive suburban development taking shape throughout the village. In the three years prior, developments of 200 to 300 (or more) homes had been started and completed at Hillside Terrace, Riviera Ridge, and Crestwood. In addition, a nine-acre shopping plaza had been completed just off of Route 25A in the eastern end of the village. (Kings Park Heritage Museum.)

Color Postcards Depicting Both an Aerial View and Boardwalk View of Sunken Meadow State Park, c. 1965. These color postcards depict the boardwalk and beach at Sunken Meadow State Park. (Aerial view photographed by Milt Price and published by Tomlin Art Company; boardwalk view published by Louis Dormand, Richard H. Handley Collection of Long Island Americana, Smithtown Library.)

GIRL SCOUTS MARCHING ON MAIN STREET, C. 1953. A local troop leader and her troop march in a summer parade in the early 1950s. They are pictured in front of the local movie theater, which opened in 1926 and was renamed Park Theater in 1941. (Kings Park Heritage Museum.)

SAUER MEAT AND TRUCK, 1957. Joseph Sauer, who lived on Hilden Street, opened his butcher and meat shop in downtown Kings Park in 1953. Fred Messina purchased the business in 1984, and he still operates a family business, the Kings Park Meat Market, at the location at 76 Main Street. (Kings Park Heritage Museum.)

AERIAL VIEW OF TANZI HARDWARE AND LUMBER COMPANY AND RAILROAD STATION, C. 1960. The Tanzi family arrived in Kings Park from Italy in the 1930s; Louis, the father of two sons, Carlo and Joseph, commuted to work at the Brooklyn Navy Yard throughout World War II. Carlo started this lumberyard, which remained in business until 1995, closing during the era of big-box hardware stores (like Home Depot) that made for a challenging economic environment for smaller family businesses. (King Pedlar Collection.)

CORNER OF THOMPSON AND OLD DOCK STREETS. Part of Kings Park's charm is based in the experience of beautiful residential areas within easy walking access of its Main Street shopping district. Four consecutive streets—Old Dock, Thompson, Henry, and Church—all run perpendicular to Main Street and include a pleasing variety of early post–World War II suburban residential architecture.

CLAYTON'S FUNERAL HOME, 1960. A funeral home at the intersection of Meadow and Indian Head Roads, this had been a livery service, run by the same family in the 19th and early 20th centuries and was also the location where local residents met in 1913 to formally begin the Kings Park Fire Department. (King Pedlar Collection.)

Longhorn Diner at the East Corner of Pulaski Road and Main Street, 1979. As Kings Park suburbanized between the 1950s and 1970s, its business district stretched farther westward. The hospital continued to be a major source of employment, but Kings Park also increasingly became home to year-round commuters who worked in New York City. This diner opened in 1954 and was the first all-night diner in the village. Numerous restaurants have operated out of the same site since. (King Pedlar Collection.)

Building That was Formerly Skipper's Bar, c. 2010. This bar was built, initially owned, and run by Pete Hildenbrand, a local resident who also worked in the plumbing shop at the Kings Park State Hospital. (King Pedlar Collection.)

AL HYDE, VETERAN, C. 2010. An Eastern Airlines pilot for 33 years, Hyde was one of a significant number of Fort Salonga/Kings Park World War II veterans. Hyde's plane went down over North Africa during the war, and he was seriously wounded. However, he returned to service and was eventually sent to the Pacific Rim, where he flew an additional 137 missions during the war. (King Pedlar Collection.)

KNIGHTS OF COLUMBUS. A Catholic-based fraternal organization, the Father Seyfried Council of the Knights of Columbus is located at 44 Church Street and has been chartered as a council since 1903, making it one of the oldest councils in New York State. The council was named after a prominent pastor at St. Joseph's Church, which is located directly across the street.

VFW Hall and Veterans Day Group, 2003. A small group of veterans came together in 1956 to form a local Veterans of Foreign Wars post, VFW No. 5796. In a short time, 200 local men came together for the initial meeting, and James D. Dempsey became the group's first commander. The VFW is now located in a building at the corner of Church Street and Veterans Lane in a building that had been previously owned by the Knights of Columbus of St. Joseph's Roman Catholic Church. (King Pedlar Collection.)

CAPT. STEVE BUTLER AND FAMILY, 2008. Steve Butler, captain of the Kings Park Fire Department in 2008, posed with his family and Santa during Christmastime in 2008. Butler was a lieutenant with the Port Authority Police Department and a responder—along with his father and a brother—at Ground Zero during 9/11. (King Pedlar Collection.)

Tim Egan (left), Leo Ostebo (center), and Marianne Howard, 2016. Ostebo has lived in Kings Park since 1958. He was a well-regarded English teacher at Kings Park High School and also the longtime director of the Kings Park Heritage Museum, which provided a number of images for this project and book.

GAIL HESSEL, 2014. Gail Sallon was born in rural Hicksville and moved to Kings Park in 1967, 11 years after her marriage to Jack Hessel, a school psychologist. Gail and Jack had two children, and she became a first grade teacher in Bay Shore. Her first passion is history, and over the years she has been especially focused on the Obadiah Smith House in Kings Park. Her research on it resulted in the book *The Obadiah Smith House* (created for the benefit of the Smithtown Historical Society, which is caretaker of the structure), and Gail remains a strong advocate for both the house and the rest of the history of Kings Park.

DAWSON HOUSE AT DAWSON AVENUE AND 140 MAIN STREET, 1980. Until it was ruined by a fire more than a decade after this picture was taken, this house was one of a small number of remnants from 19th-century Kings Park. It was constructed in 1898 and owned by Thomas Dawson Jr., a plumber at Kings Park State Hospital. Dawson raised three daughters in this home. Beginning in the 1930s, the Field family lived there; Allen, the last member of the Field family to live here, resided in the house in the 1970s. (King Pedlar Collection.)

SMITHTOWN LIBRARY, KINGS PARK BRANCH, 1968. This photograph shows the exterior of the old Kings Park Branch of The Smithtown Library located at 1 Church Street in Kings Park. (Richard H. Handley Collection of Long Island Americana, Smithtown Library; photograph by Bil Peterson.)

KINGS PARK BRANCH LIBRARY, 1968. Kings Park became the site of the first branch of the Smithtown Public Library (the community had several previous smaller libraries that operated out of the Lucien Memorial Methodist Church and a Main Street storefront). It was chartered by the New York State Board of Regents in 1955 and moved into its present building on Church Street after a $1-million expansion program that began in February 1968. (Richard H. Handley Collection of Long Island Americana, Smithtown Library.)

KINGS PARK BRANCH LIBRARY AFTER RENOVATIONS. Smithtown residents approved a referendum in 2001 that made the main library and its three other branches—including this one in Kings Park—independent. It also opened the door to much-needed system-wide renovations, which were approved in another vote in 2008. In Kings Park, remodeling began in April 2011 and was completed the following year, adding storage space in the basement and a new children's room.

OPENING OF THE BANK OF SMITHTOWN, KINGS PARK BRANCH, 1965. Smithtown town supervisor John V.N. Klein (who held the position from 1964 until 1970) attended the ribbon-cutting ceremony for the opening of a new Bank of Smithtown branch in Kings Park in 1965.

CONNOLLY'S BAR AND RESTAURANT, C. 1965. Connolly's was located at the current site of the Old Dock Inn, at the end of Old Dock Road, a restaurant that became another setting for family seafood dining in 1982. (King Pedlar Collection.)

PARK BAKE SHOP. The Park Bake Shop is located at 112 Main Street and is currently owned by Lucy and Gabe Shtanko, who have run this local institution for 14 years. Mouthwatering pastries, fresh donuts, and even wedding cakes are on the menu. This location has contained a bakery since 1984; the bakery was previously owned by Bill and Karen Saverese for 20 years.

EDELWEISS DELICATESSEN. A fixture at its location at 86 Main Street since 1990, Edelweiss is owned by the Hennings family, which has been in the delicatessen business for more than 50 years. Edelweiss carries a wide variety of foods, including German delicacies such as leberkaese, sauerbraten, and German potato salad.

Russell Savatt Village Square Town Park. This square was dedicated to the memory of Russ Savatt (1902–1992), who owned a barbershop on this site until it burned down in the early 1970s; he then moved his shop a few stores to the west and eventually retired in 1984. Savatt was a well-known local character, active in the community as the founder of the Kings Park Boys Athletic Club and a member of the Kings Park Volunteer Fire Department.

WALKING AND BIKING TRAILS. The Kings Park Hike and Bike Trail, the setting for much local area recreation, runs 1.5 miles between Old Dock Road at Church Street in Kings Park and Nissequogue River State Park. The trail shows a way that the community has injected new life into abandoned portions of the Kings Park State Hospital. The path follows what was once a railroad spur that connected to the hospital.

ASTORIA BANK. Discussions of and plans for the closing the Kings Park Psychiatric Center led to an increase in economic development in the early 1990s as the village attempted to deal with the coming transition. One of the businesses that arrived during this period was Astoria Federal Savings Bank (now Astoria Bank) at 33 Main Street.

TANZI PLAZA, KINGS PARK. After many years as the location of Tanzi Lumber, this retail center on Indian Head Road was reborn as a shopping plaza that came to include the Kings Park Hardware Company, a big-box alternative opened by Tony Tanzi in 2011 and built on the same footprint as the old lumberyard.

KINGS PARK MANOR APARTMENTS. In the last several decades, Kings Park has become the locale of a number of small affordable housing projects. This 270-unit garden apartment complex—designed for and targeted to retirees aged 55 and older—is located south of Pulaski Road and Main Street.

VIEW OF KINGS PARK CENTER LOOKING TOWARD THE RAILROAD ON CHURCH STREET. Working with Vision Long Island, Kings Park residents and community leaders have recently embraced a strong downtown revitalization plan that will include the construction of several hundred new affordable housing units, a more pedestrian-friendly Main Street with expanded curbs and better intersections, and improved overall management. At the time of the publication of this book in 2017, the planning process for this exciting future transformation was continuing to gather momentum.

DISCOVER THOUSANDS OF LOCAL HISTORY BOOKS FEATURING MILLIONS OF VINTAGE IMAGES

Arcadia Publishing, the leading local history publisher in the United States, is committed to making history accessible and meaningful through publishing books that celebrate and preserve the heritage of America's people and places.

Find more books like this at
www.arcadiapublishing.com

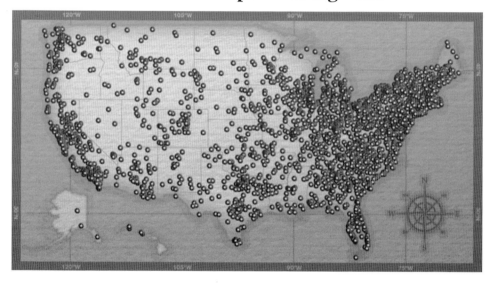

Search for your hometown history, your old stomping grounds, and even your favorite sports team.